Three Buddhists Walked Into an AA Meeting …and got sober.

"…Where perceived barriers become wisdom gates."

By Bill K.

Text Copyright © 2016 Bill K.

To the Buddhist and Buddhist-inclined who have a desire to stop drinking – and to those participating in any other 12-Step program.

Acknowledgments

Thank you to my friends who have shared their experience and wisdom, and have lent their support on many levels.

This book could not have been written without you.

Table of Contents

Preface

Foreword

Introduction

1935-1939 – Buddhists Not To Be Found

    Buddhist influence not overlooked

The Higher Power Thing

Prayer

Where Perceived Barriers Become Wisdom Gates

It Works For Us

12 & Zen

Comments

Comments From Others

A Teacher Writes

Preface

It's been a rewarding journey writing this book; but it didn't start out that way. The idea first came to me about two years ago after reading a magazine opinion piece where the author basically said that AA was not the most suitable place for Buddhists to get sober because of differences in philosophy.

This was so contrary to what I know, have experienced and seen -- so contrary to <u>my</u> opinions! Our views clashed and I found myself drawn into the tension-plagued world of opinion and judgments (whose only outcome is to produce more clashing, and less peace of mind for both parties). My practice went out the window until one day when the words "call and respond" popped into my head.

Life is an ongoing series of "call and respond". In every moment, in every thing, in every direction through all my senses, the world is calling to me – a bird singing, a vacant parking spot, a gentle touch, moonrise, someone pulling in front and taking the vacant parking spot, children laughing, a stubbed toe, puffy clouds, an upset stomach, puppy breath, smelling garlic, a stranger's smile, a rude clerk, back ache, a flat tire, a fresh tomato's juice dribbling down my chin, an opinion piece -- a never-ending list of calls.

Fast forward to a few days ago. When I was discussing this topic and an earlier draft with a friend, his response was, "I don't know." He reminded me of what I already know -- *that I don't know*. Not knowing has a way of taking the wind out of opinions' sails.

I thought of Shunryu Suzuki's classic book, *Zen Mind, Beginner's Mind*: "In the beginner's mind there are many possibilities, but in the expert's there are few." Then a koan came me: "Not knowing is most intimate." And lastly (the universe must have seen I needed additional help) I came across a quote from Jan Chozen Bays Roshi: "A wonderful aspect of Buddhist teaching is that each person is asked to be curious, to investigate and confirm from their own experience."

Curiosity, yes what a wonderful tool! One cannot be curious with a closed mind. The curious ask a lot of questions, and are not afraid to say, "I don't know."

I'm not riled anymore and have come to realize the author gave me a gift. His opinion piece was actually a blessing in disguise. I wish him well in all his recovery endeavors.

Be curious as you investigate this matter of great importance, your sobriety; and how Buddhist members in AA stay true to their practice.

Bill K. *
Summer 2016

* Because other contributors and I relate to being AA members in this book, and in respect to the AA Traditions is why I do not use last names.

Foreword

My AA program and my Zen meditation practice started almost at the same time and for this I am very grateful. It has been almost 31 years; and throughout these years I have made friends in both Zen communities and the AA program – AA friends, Zen friends, and co-practitioner friends. AA's theistic vocabulary was never a problem for me or hundreds of other Buddhists I have met along the way in AA.

Earlier this year I had the wonderful opportunity to attend a 12-step meeting in a mountain monastery. It was a great experience. Over the last few years I have been to AA meetings in a variety of Buddhist communities, Zen, Vajrayana and Vipassana.

I would encourage without hesitation anyone with a Buddhist meditation practice, whether you are a new practitioner or an old-time practitioner, to give AA a try if you have an alcohol or drug problem. There are so many meetings all over our cities and towns with the various flavors of life itself.

On a more personal note, when I went to my first AA meeting with another friend, I was scared. I also knew that I had to do *something* –this something was important because of my profound uneasiness and fear; so I just went to that evening meeting, following my friend and I didn't drink that day. The next day went to another meeting and I did not drink that day; and it continued like that for a month and I did not drink. This was astonishing for me! I knew something was going on but I did not know what it was, other than not drinking. I knew I was in the right place! This I came to know as a certain spacious-ness. At this time I started meditating with some new AA friends, generic meditation, and at the same time started re-reading the Buddhist books I had at home. For the first time I started feeling that I was coming to some elemental home. I was not clear about this something happening and as I said before, I knew that I was in the right place.

Going to meetings and doing meditation became a part of my life; and they fed each other very naturally, with some process of translating certain concepts used in AA that might have been difficult for me into my own understanding and this was somewhat spontaneous and natural. I guess the willingness to be part of what was going on was stronger than a few semantic objections. My Zen teacher encouraged me all the way in this process with incredible support, love and respect, for which I am forever grateful.

After all these years I have a favorite meeting when I am in town and my Zen practice continues strongly as ever. Zen and AA, are these two practices or one practice? Read on to discover for yourself.

Good morning! A Zen Roshi from Northern California

Introduction

Drawing from my experiences and others, it is the intent of this book to show that Buddhism and AA are wholly compatible. In fact, they wonderfully complement each other. Holding both practices can be seamlessly profound.

In 1965 Bill Wilson, one of the founders of Alcoholics Anonymous wrote, "Newcomers …represent almost every belief and attitude imaginable. We have atheists and agnostics. We have people of nearly every race, culture and religion. In A.A. we are supposed to be bound together in the kinship of a common suffering. Consequently, the full individual liberty to practice any creed or principle or therapy whatever should be a first consideration for us all. Let us not, therefore, pressure anyone with our individual or even our collective views. Let us instead accord each other the respect and love that is due to every human being as he tries to make his way toward the light. Let us always try to be inclusive rather than exclusive…"

Early on, the founding members of AA recognized that the twelve steps may not be for everyone. In the Book *Alcoholics Anonymous* (AKA The Big Book) it says that AA is not the only game in town -- it doesn't have a lock on recovery programs. No organized religion would say look elsewhere if you don't like what we offer. But how will you know if AA is not for you without giving it your best effort?

If I'm close-minded about any part of my life, my life is diminished.

Tilopa to Naropa: "Where there is attachment, there is suffering; where there is bias, there is limitation." Surya Das, *The Snow Lions Turquoise Mane*, P. 43.

For more than 80 years now, AA has a track record showing how <u>anyone</u> (this includes you) can get sober. The major hurdle is not how AA does things; the major hurdle is how an individual perceives the program. Attitude <u>is</u> everything.

Awakening comes in many forms. Getting sober is an awakening. Awakenings can occur at any time, place, or situation – even in AA meetings.

1935-1939, Buddhists Not To Be Found

"Buddhism" isn't mentioned in the original Big Book at all. It's no wonder some Buddhists today feel their spiritual path was overlooked.

The Big Book was written as a reflection of the U.S. culture of the mid to late 1930s. In 1940, 91% of the U.S. population identified themselves Christian. It's only until the second edition came out in 1955 where it mentions "…a sprinkling of Moslems and Buddhists" are members. Buddhism was just beginning to become known to the public. Even today in the U.S., as far as religions are represented, Buddhists comprise only 0.7%.

We know that AA began in 1935; and apparently there weren't any Buddhists amongst the first 100 members when the book of *Alcoholics Anonymous* was being written. Buddhist philosophy never made it into the book.

Some say the Big Book has an archaic writing style that is not suitable for today's readers. Remember, they were writing for the 1939 audience. Their lives and society, in some ways, were very different than today. It's their conveyed message that's universal and applicable. When books are old or the writing style different, do we stop reading them? Or do we dig deeper to understand the story and how it relates to my life today?

Think of the Big Book as a meeting in print. Bill Wilson and the first 100 people in AA are simply telling us their stories and sharing their experiences. We read how they failed – we read how they got sober – we read about the things they did to stay sober. "Take what you want and leave the rest" attitude goes a long way in forming one's personal path to sobriety.

> "Each thing by nature has worth,
> but we notice it is shaped by its circumstances.
> Things fit together like boxes and lids,
> while the absolute is like arrows meeting in mid-air."
> Shitou xiqian, From *Taking Part in the Gathering*

Living life on life's terms; isn't that what practice is about? If you practice a 12-Step tradition and a Buddhist tradition, these are not separate vehicles. I look at them as riding in the same vehicle.

I see and hear it all the time, in meeting after meeting, people telling me how it was for them early on, as newcomers and first seeing the Steps on the wall, or hearing the word "God" spoken, or saying the Lord's Prayer at the end of a meeting – All of these *perceived barriers*, have caused people to leave.

> How sad that people ignore the near
> and search for truth afar,
> like someone in the midst of water

crying out in thirst,
like a child of a wealthy home
wandering among the poor.

Praise Song for Meditation – Hakuin Ekaku

Then there are the ones who stay and follow a few suggestions. They stay long enough to see what happens when they let go of judgments and opinions. They stay long enough for wisdom gates to appear; and their lives are changed for the better.

Anytime I let go of something – really let it go – "it" goes elsewhere outside of myself, allowing the Universe to have its way with it.

"We can only clear the ground a bit. If our testimony helps sweep away prejudice, enables you to think honestly, encourages you to search diligently within yourself, then, if you wish, you can join us on the Broad Highway. With this attitude you cannot fail. The consciousness of your belief is sure to come to you." P.55 We Agnostics Chapter

Buddhist Influence Not Overlooked

Yes, it would have made it a lot easier for Buddhists today if there had been some Buddhists among the first 100 AA members offering input in the writing of the Big Book. But Buddhist philosophy made it into AA far earlier than most realize. What if I told you, by citing a 1940s AA pamphlet (commissioned by Dr. Bob no less), you could begin chanting the Eightfold Path at your meeting?

I learned of some early pamphlets that were printed in the 1940s, "Dr. Bob, the co-founder of A.A., was responsible for these Akron Pamphlets." One pamphlet in particular, *Spiritual Milestones in Alcoholics Anonymous*, has a jewel within for Buddhists:

Consider the eight-part program laid down in Buddhism: Right view, right aim, right speech, right action, right living, right effort, right mindedness and right contemplation. The Buddhist philosophy, as exemplified by these eight points, could be literally adopted by AA as a substitute or an addition to the Twelve Steps.
Generosity, universal love and welfare of others rather than consideration of self are basic to Buddhism.

I was overwhelmed to see Buddhist "scripture", the Eightfold Path, mentioned in the early years of A.A. Just imagine, had there been Buddhists members among the first 100 people of A.A., the Eightfold Path might well have been integrated into the Big Book and offered as an alternative to the Twelve Steps. Then again, if you pay attention to the message of the Big Book, Buddhist philosophy is presented throughout.

Just imagine, had there been some Buddhists among the first 100 members, surely texts such as the Eightfold Path would have been integrated into the Big Book! This would have made AA more accepting to the early Buddhist alcoholics. And later when the *Twelve Steps and Twelve Traditions* book was published, the Eightfold Path might have been printed along with the St. Francis Prayer.

The evidence is in this Akron Pamphlet. No longer can others say AA is not for Buddhists. Buddhist philosophy found its way into AA literature long ago. We now have proof from our AA ancestors, a validation and approval that AA and Buddhism can be practiced successfully together. There are Buddhists who've been doing this for many years. In the *Spiritual Milestones in Alcoholics Anonymous* pamphlet it states, "… The Twelve Steps of AA give us a program of dynamic action…" Right action indeed with the inclusion of the Eightfold Path!

The Higher Power Thing

It is suggested that we find a God of our own understanding. This is how the Big Book was written, through the eyes, consciousness and concept of the first 100 (or so) members.

"God"…it's just the name some others call their Higher Power. I read the Big Book through the eyes, consciousness and concept of my Higher Power. We are not to be concerned with anyone else's Higher Power, only our own.

We are pilgrims, where is your life taking you today?

"The phrase 'God as we understand him' is perhaps the most important expression to be found in our whole AA vocabulary. Within the compass of these five significant words there can be included every kind and degree of faith, together with the positive assurance that each of us may choose his own." (Bill W. Language of the Heart)

What part "of your own understanding" isn't being understood?

Usually, in order to become a member of mainstream Christian churches, one must vow to believe in God, Jesus, and the Holy Spirit. AA's Tradition Three states: "The only requirement for AA membership is a desire to stop drinking." In AA, the choice is yours, to believe or not believe in something; and the people about you pretty much don't care who or what you have chosen. To some it can be a deity. To others it's relying upon something other than a deity:

>"My concept of a higher power is the power of good."

>Pasadena, Calif., April 1978
>"The Power of Good,"
>*Spiritual Awakenings*

Came to believe.
Came to believe what?
I don't know.

Dizang asked Fayan, "Where are you going"
Fayan said, "Around on a pilgrimage."
Dizang asked, "What is the purpose of your pilgrimage?"
Fayan said, "I don't know."
Dizan said, "Not knowing is most intimate."

One of my teachers often says, "Zen does not require that you believe in anything."

Some members consider AA their own personal religion. It's a religion only as much as you'd like it to be as it relates to your spiritual practice.

I once read where Shunryu Suzuki Roshi was asked, "What do you believe in?"
He replied, "I believe in the dharma."

"I realized that it is possible to believe in a Higher Power, in the efficacy of prayer and meditation, in making a conscious contact with a Higher Power as those concepts, privately understood - or not understood - are suggested in AA, without the loss of one iota of my precious identity."

> New York, N.Y., September 1977
> "AA and the Religious Turnoff"
> *Spiritual Awakenings*

Do I trust my God? If this is difficult for you to answer, then ask, "Do I trust my life?" Two questions are being asked here – or are they ultimately the same question?

"Spiritual growth and experiences are not limited to orthodox believers in a deity, any more than the disease of alcoholism is limited to skid-row bums."

> Casper, Wyo., September 1969
> "Is 'Agnostic' a Nasty Word?", *AA Grapevine*

The Big Book's "…main object is to enable you to find a Power greater than yourself which will solve your problem" P. 45 -- a power of your own understanding. This includes higher power realm(s) that are completely outside the mind-set of those who helped write the Big Book.

In Buddhism we hear about *vehicles*, in the simplest of terms, moving from one place to another as a function of our practice.

What if (bear with me please) it was suggested in a stranger-than-life Big Book that we all find an automobile of our own understanding and it implied it be a Buick?

- Person A: But I don't like Buicks. [Then choose a different car to take you places.]
- Person B: I don't like cars at all. I own a horse. [If your horse works for your mode of transportation, good for you.]
- Person C: Autos pollute. And the upkeep on a horse is too much for me. I'm happy to be walking. [Walking will get you to your spiritual destination just as effectively as other modes of transportation.]
- Person D: I'm bedridden and cannot ride or walk. Am I doomed? [Rely on the formless vehicle you were born with.]

The Big Book is a *vehicle* of sorts. "To us, the Realm of Spirit is broad, roomy, all inclusive; never exclusive or forbidding..." P. 46

"… The main problem of the alcoholic center in his mind…" P. 23

A sponsee asked me about my Higher Power. Then he questioned me how my Higher Power, not a deity per se, would work for me. I stopped him there and said, "It's none of my business what he or others think of my Higher Power. It has <u>everything</u> to do with what <u>I think</u> of my Higher Power." We don't apologize to anyone about our Higher Power.

Prayer

AA suggests that prayer is useful. Finding your way is not difficult. I'll bet you have prayed without even knowing it.

How far can you point your finger? Spend a few minutes working on your pointing skills. Point to something near by; next midrange; through to the other side of that car; now do a long-range point. You can even point through walls. We find we're already pretty good at this skill. Can our pointing be infinite? I think so –pointing is infinite.

Now sit back and think of things and such you are grateful for. Out loud say "Thank you" for what you are grateful for. After these words have left your lips, they cannot be retrieved. They've been cast out into the cosmos, just like your pointing. I call this a grateful thanks prayer. It's so easy, almost too easy.

Vajrayana teacher Elizabeth Mattis-Namgyel said, "It doesn't matter if you don't know whom you're praying to. The very act of asking for help allows the heart to open and invite the world in."

"We recite vows, "…which are a kind of prayer-wrapped intention," writes Jan Chozen Bays Roshi.

Prayer is not foreign to Buddhists. Hannah Tennant-Moore writes: "Tibetans recite mantras to invite help from various deities, and millions of people throughout East Asia recite the name of Amitabha Buddha in the hope of being reborn in the Pure Land. For thousands of years, the *paritta* suttas ('the discourses for protection') have been recited in Theravada countries as protection against all kinds of dangers, from disease to snakes. Even the most basic Buddhist practices – metta meditation ('May all beings be happy and well'), the bodhisattva vow ('May I attain enlightenment for the benefit of all beings'), and the vows of refuge ('I take refuge in the Buddha, dharma, and sangha') – contain a spirit of invocation." ("Buddhism's Higher Power", *Tricycle* Spring 2016)

Find *your* way to pray. Be creative, use your imagination, follow your heart – it's your choice, not the choice of others.

"I chose to set aside my fears and just let see what happened," said Christine S., Tibetan Buddhist nun with 31 years of sobriety, only to discover that A.A. though theistic in language is clearly not theistic in spirit." At a meeting I remember Christine telling us, "My god is not a noun; my higher power is a verb."

One's higher power does not have to be God! I think of my Higher Power in different ways -- at times it's simply the Universe, or the dharma (as in cosmic law and order), and other times the Three Treasures:

26

The Buddha (the historical Buddha or Buddha nature), the Dharma (the teachings), and the Sangha (the community). Finding a Buddhist higher power is as simple as this.

Impossible to describe, the following points in the *direction* of my Higher Power.

We have a meeting where a person in the audience is asked to read a passage of their choice from the Big Book; on this particular day Lisa S. read: "Acceptance is the key to my relationship with God today. I never just sit and do nothing while waiting for Him to tell me what to do. Rather, I do whatever is in front of me to be done, and I leave the results up to Him; however it turns out, that's God's will for me." (P. 420)

That's it! This is how I, as a Zen Buddhist in AA relate to my Higher Power: <u>Acceptance</u> is the key to my relationship with the Universe today. I never just sit and do nothing while waiting for the Dharma to tell me what to do. Rather, I do whatever is in front of me to be done, and leave the results up to the Universe; however it turns out, that's the Dharma in my life. I like what Layman Pang said, "Collecting firewood and carrying water are prayers that reach the gods."

"God, I offer myself to Thee…" (P. 63), this is the beginning of the Third Step prayer. And since my Higher Power is not a "Thee", no problem -- I like to tell people my Higher Power is phenomenal! I live in a phenomenal universe.

Some but not all meetings end with saying the Lord's Prayer. This is a time for inclusiveness. We are not forced to say this prayer. I say it out loud. I'm adding my voice to the collective common good; and realize that this meeting has chosen to say the prayer.

"The power in these rooms is greater than the sum total of those of us present."

Lodi, Calif., March 1987
The Beat Goes On", The Home Group: Heartbeat of AA

All the people holding hands; there is a singleness of purpose taking place with this ritual and a room full of Bodhisattvas. Close your eyes. You don't have to speak the words – soak in this time for loving-kindness.

We do not need to forgo our practice while others are reciting the Lord's Prayer. Consider creating your own prayer, perhaps something like this:

The Lord's Prayer
A Buddhist's Prayer

Our Father who art in heaven,
All Buddhas throughout space and time.

Hallowed be thy Name.
I bow to you.

Thy kingdom come,
Thy will be done,
On earth as it is in heaven.
I take refuge in Buddha
I take refuge in Dharma
I take refuge in Sangha

Give us this day our daily bread.
We give thanks to all the ancestors of meditation in the still halls...

And forgive us our trespasses,
As we forgive those who trespass against us.
All the ancient twisted karma
From beginningless greed hatred and ignorance, Born of my body, mouth and thought, I now confess openly and fully.

And lead us not into temptation,
But deliver us from evil.
My actions are my only true belongings. I cannot escape the consequences of my actions.

For thine is the kingdom,
And the power, and the glory
Forever and ever.
How boundless and free is the sky of Samadhi, how bright the full moon of wisdom. Is

anything missing now? **Nirvana is right here, before our eyes...**

 Amen (It means, "so be it.")

 In the Bible, Luke 6:30, Jesus says "Do to others as you would have them do to you." This is the *Golden Rule* and is referred to in the Big Book as love thy neighbor as thyself. This is a transcending prayer.

 What would Buddha say?
 "Do no harm."

 A local Zen community has a newspaper ad saying, "Zen is Life!" Taped to my shower wall is a quote from one of my teachers, "This is your life right now."

 What is Zen?
  Attention! Attention! Attention!
 What is AA?
  Attention! Attention! Attention!

 To the Buddhist or like-minded alcoholic, may your practice thrive in AA.
 To the non-Buddhist alcoholic, here is but another example of AA's welcome availability to all.
 Gratitude: Where the glass is half full even when it's empty.

Where Perceived Barriers Become Wisdom Gates

This story, *Not Far from Buddhahood* (Page 36, Zen Flesh, Zen Bones – Reps & Senzaki) shows Gasan listening to words from the Bible and acknowledging a Buddhist response.

A university student while visiting Gasan asked him: "Have you ever read the Christian Bible?"

"No, read it to me," said Gasan.

The student opened the Bible and red from St. Matthew: "And why take ye thought for raiment [clothing]? Consider the lilies of the field, how they grow. They toil not, neither do they spin, and yet I say unto you that even Solomon in all his glory was not arrayed like one of these. ...Take therefore no thought for the morrow, for the morrow shall take thought for the things of itself."

Gasan said: "Whoever uttered those words I consider an enlightened man."

The student continued reading: "Ask and it shall be given you, seek and ye shall find, knock and it shall be opened unto you. For everyone that asketh receiveth, and he that seeketh findeth, and to him that knocketh, it shall be opened."

Gasan remarked: "That is excellent. Whoever said that is not far from Buddhahood."

You might think the Big Book has nothing to offer for the Buddhist alcoholic. Really? The Big Book was written <u>by</u> alcoholics, <u>for</u> alcoholics. These are my people. Are you saying you can't find *your* story and practice within?

Many have found their own way to participate fully in AA while holding true to their Buddhist path.

"…We have stopped fighting anybody or anything." P. 103

There is no value in criticizing the Big Book on how it was written almost 80 years ago. I've heard people complain about having to re-interpret the Big Book to align with their Buddhist principles. Oh my, what a dull life this world would be if we were only spoon-fed what we wanted to hear or read.

In the last chapter of this book (12 & Zen) I go into more detail in how koans, used in a non-traditional way, can be melded with the 12-Steps. Here's an example of how a koan opens one's view of AA.

Case 40 from <u>The Gateless Barrier</u>, *Kuei-shan Kicks Over the Water Bottle*

When Kuei-shan was with Pai-chang's assembly, he was cook of the monastery. Pai-chang wanted to choose a founding teacher for Mount Ta-kuei. He invited all his monks to make a presentation, saying, "The outstanding one will be sent." Then he took a water bottle and set it on the floor, and said, "Don't call this a water bottle. What would you call it?"

The head monk said, "It can't be called a wooden clog."

Pai-chang then asked Kueh-shan his opinion. Kuei-shan kicked over the water bottle and walked out.

Pai'chang laughed and said, "The head monk loses." Kueh-shan thereupon was made the founding teacher at Mount Ta-kuei.

Sit with this koan for a while and think about the times you merely label things vs. when you're paying attention and engaged in matters.

Here's the same koan in an AA setting:

A group was having difficulty in choosing between two people who would be the next secretary. A Big Book was placed on the table. "Don't call this the Big Book. What would you call it?"

Rick replied, "This is not the AA Bible." He felt pretty confident with his response because the Big Book is often referred to as the AA textbook.

Now it was Patty's turn to respond. She took the book and launched it into the air like a paper airplane, singing the words, "Fly me to the moon."

Rick's response was intellectual. Patty's response demonstrated a grand gesture of how life is unpredictable and full of uncertainty. Patty became the next secretary.

Wisdom gates afford us every opportunity to see things as they are in relation to our practice -- the Big Book we're holding in our hands offers us myriad wisdom gates.

I have found many examples of Buddhist principles throughout the Big Book. In the first 164 pages I've underlined close to 200 phrases, sentences and paragraphs that resonate with my Zen practice. My first idea was for a larger book, documented all these excerpts with my commentary or like-minded Buddhists writings.

Since I wanted to be above board, I contacted the AA Central Office and explained the concept of this book; but they had a bit of a problem over me including 200+ quotes from the Big Book. Now you're reading my Plan B.

I offer some examples; first the Big Book quote, followed by my response:

- I was **to test my thinking by the new God-consciousness within**… Page 13

- I was to **sit quietly** when in doubt … 13

Remember, this is the God or Higher Power of *your* understanding, whoever or whatever that force may be, powerful beyond comprehension.

"When knowing stops, when thoughts about who we are fall away, vast space opens up and our kinship with every living thing is revealed. Joy appears. All this originates from the ocean of essential nature. It is beyond explanation, we just accept it with respect and gratitude. Anything that gets in the way of understanding this is a cause of suffering and something to refrain from. Moment by moment, thought appears, the earth appears; we appear. When we touch each bit of life against this great heart, we find we cannot reject any single thing. With our virtues, our failures, and our imperfections, this is the body we take refuge in; this is our offering. From CityZen Refuge Ceremony

- Faith has to work twenty-four hours a day in and through us, **or we perish**. Page 16

"Walking the Way, we're never near or far from it: deluded, we are cut off from it by mountains and rivers. You who seek the mystery, in daylight or in the shadows of night, don't throw away your time." From

<u>Taking Part in the Gathering</u> – Shitou xiqian (CityZen)

- We feel that elimination of our drinking **is but a beginning**. P. 19

I have a friend, Barbara, who tells how she used to love to drink and think, and eventually she realized she had a *thinking problem*. We do. Our problems lie in our minds, for which meditation and our practice offer great benefits.

"The battle of likes and dislikes –
   this is the disease of the mind.
Misunderstanding the great mystery
   people labor in vain for peace.
Mind is perfect like vast space
   nothing lacking and nothing extra."
From <u>Relying on Mind</u> – Seng-t'san (CityZen)

- Actually we were fooling ourselves, **for deep down in every man, woman, and child, is the fundamental idea of God**. 55

- **We found the Great Reality** deep down within us. 55

#28 Open Your Own Treasure House

Daiju visited the master Baso in China. Baso asked: "What do you seek?"

"Enlightenment," replied Daiju.

"You have your own treasure house. Why do you search outside?" Baso asked.

Daiju inquired: "Where is my treasure house?"

Baso answered: What you are asking is your treasure house."

Daiju was enlightened! Ever after he urged his friends: "Open your own treasure house and use those treasures." (Zen Flesh Zen Bones –Reps & Senzaki)

- Our real purpose is to fit ourselves to be of maximum service to God and the people about us. P. 77

Part of my daily ritual is to remind myself that everything I need today is right here. I have to pay attention, be aware of things, give more and take less, and wherever I am, whomever I'm with or whatever I'm doing, may I contribute the greater good.

- Step 2: Came to believe that a Power greater than ourselves could restore us to sanity.

From *The Record of Transmitting the Light*, Jayata, the 20th Ancestor is talking to the 19th ancestor Kumarata. "For a long time, I have taken refuge in the Buddhadharma. Relying on the power of the Dharma…"

- Step 5: Admitted to God, to ourselves, and to another human being the exact nature of our wrongs.

> "All the ancient twisted karma
> From beginningless greed, hatred and ignorance
> Born of my body, mouth and thought
> I now confess openly and fully
> <u>Purification Sutra</u>" (CityZen)

- Step 7: Humbly asked Him to remove our shortcomings.

In the 12x12, Step Seven Chapter, it says, "…the attainment of greater humility is the foundation principle of each of AA's Twelve Steps."

Buddhism sees humility as a virtue, where only a humble mind can readily recognize its own "defilements" (or as we say shortcomings and character defects).

"When the spirit is all purged of its filth accumulated from time immemorial, it stands naked with no trappings. It is now empty, free, genuine, assuming its native authority. And there is a joy in this, not the kind of joy which is liable to be upset by its counterpart grief, but an absolute joy which is the gift of God, which makes a man enjoy good in all his labour, and which nothing can be taken, to which nothing can be put, but which shall stay forever." D. T. Suzuki

- We are going to know a **new freedom and a new happiness**. P. 83

    Verse of the Kesa:

    "I wear the robe of freedom,
    The bare field, the blessings,
    The teachings of the Tathagata,
    Saving all the many beings." (CityZen)

- We absolutely insist on **enjoying life**. P. 132

    "Every morning, when we wake up, we have twenty-four brand-new hours to live. What a precious gift! We have the capacity to live in a way that these twenty-four hours will bring peace, joy, and happiness to ourselves and others."
    - Thich Nhat Hanh

- He will be at the **jumping off place**. P. 152

    Koan: Master Sekiso said, "How will you step forward from the top of a hundred-foot pole?" Case 46 - The Gateless Gate

    Waiting for the world to give me only what I prefer is going to be a long wait. Jump!

    My AA program is open and strong; and because of this my AA practice finds AA messages in

Buddhist texts and philosophy. My Buddhist practice is strong; and because of this, my Zen practice finds Buddhist messages and philosophy in the Big Book.

"We are sure God wants us to be happy, joyous, and free." (P. 133) Since I'm at total ease with a Higher Power of my own understanding, this passage in the Big Book is a reflection of "…singing and dancing are the voice of the Law" from the sutra, *Praise Song For Meditation – Hakuin Ekaku*. They both have a grounding influence on my practice.

It's not about trying to reinterpret the Big Book. If our practice is strong, messages, wisdom gates appear.

Some read into the Big Book that it's pushing a Christian agenda. Not so. In AA's formative years it adopted some but not all of the tenets of the evangelical Oxford Group. What was not carried over to AA was the promotion of Jesus and the Bible. People were not staying sober in the Oxford Group. They were devout Christians (Dr. Bob being one of them) who were helping to write the Big Book, and they knew if AA was to survive, it had to be open to ALL views, not just Christian views.

AA is not a religion. The Big Book states this in different ways. The book is meant to be suggestive it says. It also says we are "not allied with any particular faith, sect or denomination." There's no

AA pope or leader in charge. AA is a spiritual program, that's compatible with the human spirit.

Why is it that some Jewish rabbis and Christian priests and ministers take up a Zen practice? It is so they can deepen their faith. I also think they realize, in the big picture, the two religions have more in common than differences.

Buddhist: "How does one do Christianity?"
Christian: "By turning worry into Wonder."
Buddhist: "Ah, hard practice!"

AA does not ask you to dilute your spiritual practice; instead, it invites people from all religious practices to participate.

In 1961, A.A. co-founder Bill W. wrote: "…our concepts of a higher power and God as we understand him afford everyone a nearly unlimited choice of spiritual belief and action."

Buddhists have practiced their way through countless difficulties, wars, rebellions, famines, disease, despots, and purges – and still some Buddhists say AA doesn't work for them. What I've found in my nearly 30 years of sobriety and 20 years practicing Zen Buddhism is that the book of *Alcoholics Anonymous* reflects countless examples of Buddhist philosophy, even though it's written in the language and culture of 1939 USA, where 91% of the people identified themselves as Christian.

It Works For Us

Upon finding AA, via a treatment center, I've stayed sober. Things were working pretty well for me for about eight years, even without a meditation practice.

For a couple of years I had the feeling that something was missing. It became apparent that the missing part was meditation, so I began reading, for a year or so, every single issue of the three most popular Buddhist magazines. Reading about Buddhism and meditation is not meditation.

Then at 10 years sobriety I found Zen and meditation. Very early on in my practice I looked around the zendo one evening. There were 32 people. Eight I knew or recognized from AA meetings. "This is going to work," I told myself.

Bob C. (29 years sober)

The last section of stories in the Big Book is entitled, "They Lost Nearly All." *"Most had taken shattering losses on nearly every front of life."* My friend Bob C. once told me, "I would be in this section of the book." In his twenties, he couldn't stay sober; his mind was like a bucking bronco. Instead of prescription drugs, a doctor prescribed that he go to a local Zen Center and learn how to meditate. For some unknown reason he followed his doctor's orders.

His early Zen practice was gnarly and out of control (bucking bronco Zen?), yet he stayed and occasionally found himself at AA meetings. God, the Steps, Sponsors, rooms filled with mostly happy people, holding hands at the end, and saying the Lord's Prayer were revolting to him. He wasn't ready.

Today he writes, "Having spent many years in Buddhist study and practice, I flat out rejected AA and its god and prayer tenets. Then, in my early thirties, I hit bottom and came face to face with my alcoholism. Somehow I ended up in AA, and eventually realized how inclusive it really is. I no longer rejected AA's suggestions because of my beliefs. I was allowed to work out my own path. That was 29 years ago; AA and Buddhism are still the foundations of my life."

From Maureen Ann M., Getzville, New York
Share Your Wisdom, Shambhala Sun, May 2015
"Several months into AA a man said to me, 'I see you're having trouble with the Higher Power concept. Maybe I could tell you what works for me.' He talked about his tour of duty in Viet Nam, about meeting Buddhist monks, learning how to meditate, having compassion. I wanted the calm my friend had. Fast-forward twenty-eight years. I'm still sober. My Higher Power is rooted in Kwan Yin, the Goddess of Compassion, and I'm walking the Eightfold Path."

Roger H. (21 years sober)

Twenty years sober, who lives by the tenets of Buddhist traditions, told me, "Early on… having patiently waded through my resentment of A.A.'s clear and apparent Christian God peer pressure, I knew God was nothing but a delusion; I am an atheist. Today, the ultimate purpose of my spiritual practice is to uncover and make contact with my essentially pure nature." Roger has found his higher power!

Tom C. (33 years sober)

With 35 years of sobriety, Tom writes, "A.A. and Buddhism -- as I've encountered it -- are gloriously compatible. To me, being sidetracked by A.A.'s often Christian-influenced vocabulary risks missing out on the inner, wordless, powerfully healing music, whose truth can't be defined with human words. Both A.A. and Buddhism are technologies in some sense. In my experience, Buddhism is a marvelous technology for experiencing the universe's music, and A.A. is an empirically efficient technology for getting us in good enough shape that we can hope to hear anything besides the incessant rumblings and shrieks of our addiction."

Dale H. (31 years sober)

Without ever seeing the Akron Pamphlets, Dale has been applying the Eightfold Path to the 12-Steps for many years. He finds this a very simple and effective way to practice.

Steps 1, 2, and 3 are about relinquishing control. He relates this to Wisdom Training -- Right View and Right Intentions (or aim).

Steps 4, 5, 6, 7, 8, and 9 are about transcending self. He relates these Steps to Ethics Training -- Right Speech, Right Action, and Right Livelihood (or living).

Steps 10, 11, and 12 are about Living Consciously. He relates these to Meditation Training -- Right Effort, Right Mindfulness (mindedness) and Right Concentration (or contemplation).

Helen V. (25 years sober)

I have a very personal bond with AA and Zen Buddhism. I discovered Zen meditation through my association with Alan Watts, and later the San Francisco Zen Center. Here was a meditation practice that expressed a similar approach to meditation, sitting still and going within (my terms for it) and letting my mind be what it is, thoughts and images in and out, letting go, letting it happen, not attaching value to any of it. Except that, and here's the surprise to me, nuggets appear. They are awareness, gifts, gems, and jewels in the seas of life for me to ponder. Sometimes they are abrasive, nagging (I must need to ferret out what wrong I have done…) and sometimes they are valuable insights, either way they represent steps to solving some hidden secret, good or bad or neutral.

Sort of struck dumb by the power of the unconscious mind, I never stopped using meditation whenever I needed it, to unravel my thoughts, worries, upheavals in my life, and began to use alcohol for the same reasons I was using meditation. It seems to me that my addiction, which wanted top billing in my life, prevented me from ever reaching the same level of meaning as in that first experience in my late twenties. Although I continued meditating, the direct connection to my collective unconscious was never potently made. At long last I entered AA, and it is there in the twelve steps I found the structure set out for me to use my meditative practice in the most powerful form. And so my "higher power" became the "collective unconscious" brought to me by my old friend from psychology, Dr. Jung. And it is in meditation that AA and Zen Buddhism make perfect counterparts to both my relief from addiction and emotional balance. The God concept was never an issue; I never even thought of calling my higher power God.

Joanie L. (27 years sober)

By the age of 32, having suffered deep betrayal, I found myself with an anchor of self- destruction around my neck, fueled by anger, resentment and self-loathing. I found myself sinking deeper into the dark abyss of depression. I used alcohol to numb the pain and eventually it began to use me. I hated it, and even worse I hated myself even more for being so weak. I began to consider a permanent ending to this painful life.

Was there anything that I even liked about myself? Looking deeply inside I saw but a tiny speck of light behind the darkness. I began to see that no matter what happened to me, or what I told myself, I still had love in my heart. No matter what, I still "loved".

Finding my way to AA via a rehab center I waded my way through the Twelve Steps. When I actually worked the steps I began to find my way to Truth. Still, I questioned the existence of God so I had a difficult time with this "Higher Power" thing. The Christianity that seemed sprinkled throughout the Big Book turned me off. But I kept working the steps. And when I came to the 11th step *"Sought through prayer and meditation"*, I found that meditation was a tremendous help with my depression and the answer to finding ME again. And in finding my way to a loving place with myself again I felt the "spiritual awakening" of the twelfth step. That spark of love that I saw inside myself <u>is my higher power</u> and is what connects me to this world. I also became more convinced, despite my earlier opinions, that AA is not a Christian group. AA is open to all. The only requirement is the desire to stop drinking.

This spiritual awakening led me to a meditation center and a Buddhist Teacher, which led me to my Bodhisattva vows, that led me to opening a meditation center 20 years later.

Following *The Eightfold Path* I can clearly see that these **Three Qualities** of Buddhism have everything in common with the Twelve Steps:

1.) Wisdom: *Right View, Right Thought,*
2.) Morality: *Right Speech, Right Action, Right Livelihood*
3.) Meditation: *Right Effort, Right Mindfulness, Right Contemplation*

I have found that each of the Twelve Steps and the Buddha's teachings have direct parallels. Both The Steps and The Path are all about **Truth** and **Acceptance**. Practicing meditation and mindfulness and putting the steps into action are about ultimate freedom and the exuberance that this freedom is accessible to all.

The object is to bring my practice into every aspect of my life – when I do this, my life becomes practice. Right now becomes practice no matter what is happening.

Retreating Resentments – My 12 & Zen in Action (Bill K. 29 years sober)

When my 12 & Zen group met in May, I posted Step 5 and the koan we used; but I didn't have time to write a commentary because I was off to a five-day sesshin (Zen Retreat). What follows is an example of how my 12 & Zen practice came to my rescue, saved me from certain angst, and provided me a rejuvenated outlook of "having joy in each other's joy."

I had been sitting for about a day with the following two koans from a second cycle of the 5 ranks of Dongshan, koans that Daiun Harada had added to his curriculum in the early 20th century. They are a separate series of poems of Dongshan, not originally linked to the first series.

- #4. Enlightenment of all beings

"Ordinary beings and Buddhas don't mingle together.
Mountains are naturally high, waters are naturally deep.
The infinite distinctions, the endless differences show –
where partridges sing, the flowers are in bloom."

- #5. Enlightenment upon enlightenment

"When your head sprouts horns, you can't stand it anymore,

When you think "I'll seek the Buddha," it's time to watch out.

In the era of emptiness, the view is clear, there is no one to see – why go south in search of the sages?"

I was soaking in these two koans, feeling closeness to them as the lid fits its appropriate box, and asking myself, "Is anything missing now?"

Then, while up in my room, just before we were to meet again in the zendo for a talk, I took a peek at my iPad, mainly to see if there was a message from my wife. There was.

"Missing you...mostly my part at this moment is with the girl [our dog] snoring softly next to me. XXXOOO to you on your cushion.

Sweet.

Then I noticed a message from my blog, a comment from someone, so I took a look.

AntHill (Not the name used) has left a new comment on your post:

*"I bought your book, * but seeing the different versions of the TWELVE STEPS, I donated it to Goodwill. I have been in the Program, since 1981. It's curious
that only the Buddhists deem it necessary to always offer different versions of the twelve steps, some sects actually rewriting*

them. *Why don't y'all rewrite the ten commandments, but that won't happen, will it? Your book STINKS of ZEN. To put it plainly, you are shitting down our backs, and calling it chocolate pudding! You are confusing a simple thing."*

* Twelve & Zen – Where the 12 Steps Meet Zen Koans

Oh my… I thought, "How did he ever draw this conclusion?" The bell rang. I needed to hurry downstairs to the zendo for the afternoon talk. I felt a resentment brewing…and gaining momentum.

Early in Megan's talk I heard the words, "…we all have Buddha-nature." I gazed about the room and thought, "I do have Buddha-nature; everyone in this room has Buddha-nature; even, even, even AntHill has Buddha-nature! How did that thought pop into my mind? He does have Buddha-nature, and with that thought I could feel the supports being kicked out from under the resentment platform I was building. What transpired was even more amazing.

- One of the earlier koans kicked in: "When your head sprouts horns, you can't stand it anymore." How quickly resentments appear, under all conditions.
- Next Torei Enji appeared in his Bodhisattva's Vow: Even though someone may be a fool, we can be compassionate. If someone turns against us, speaking ill of us and treating us bitterly,

it's best to bow down: this is the Buddha appearing to us, finding ways to free us from our own attachments – the very ones that have made us suffer again and again and again."

These were not mere words. Flowing over me like warm honey, I felt the Buddha and realized what was shone to me. This resentment left me. Even when I tried to bring it up, each feeble effort wouldn't stick to anything. There were no ill feelings toward anymore.

The next day during the "Remembrance" sutra, the Chant Leader ends with, "We especially dedicate our service to: *(each person in the room speaks names of personal dedications).* It's incredibly moving and powerful to speak out loud the names of people I care about to hear the names being spoken by others. Without thinking I heard myself say, "AntHill."

I truly wish him the greater good and thanked him for what he gave to me at this retreat, and to realize his generosity by giving the book to the Goodwill.

Regarding AntHill's comments about my book, perhaps he missed where I wrote, "If you are in a Twelve Step program, any 12 Step program, then this little book is for you."

And, "...what I offer here is <u>not</u> a substitute for an official 12 Step meeting nor a replacement of working the Steps with a sponsor."

"But included here are two other versions of the 12 Steps. I think you will see the value in them, especially when speaking to a mixed audience." By mixed audience I mean people in and out of 12-Step programs. Some people are just curious. When I introduce 12 and Zen to an audience, I make it very clear that what we are doing is not an AA meeting.

Yes, AA put together the Twelve Steps, borrowing a little here and a little there from other sources. We know that working these 12 Steps can bring joy and fulfillment to lives. Why shouldn't people who are not alcoholics or addicts benefit from a version of the 12 Steps?

May the next reader(s) of that book find what I have found – that koans will help broaden their relationship with the 12 Steps.

In the Big Book of *Alcoholics Anonymous*, the contributors emphasized the importance of reading the book with an open mind by including the warning paragraph about *contempt prior to investigation*. There's an old Zen saying, "Don't disparage the sky by looking at it through a tube." This is exactly the same way I hope you would read my book, by looking for the greatest possibilities with a big mind.

Student: What is Zen?
Teacher: It's alive!
Sponsee: What is AA?
Sponsor: It's alive!

It's my practice that brings me happiness, joy, and freedom. Thank you AntHill for your gift. Isn't it great to be alive?

12 & Zen

Today my practice is a fusion of AA and Zen. There is no separation...I cannot practice one without the other. It's an example of the Zen philosophy of *not one not two*. First I worked the Steps; now I find times where the Steps are working me. I meet with my Zen teacher to further my koan practice; now I find the koans working in my life.

Put another way, the 12-Steps plus my Zen practice equals an outcome greater than the sum.

Coming back – it's all about coming back to my practice...my 12-Step practice, my Buddhist practice, my meditation practice. As Step 12 says, "we practice these principles in all our affairs."

It was about four years ago, a Wednesday morning, it came to me while walking our dog – the koan we sat with a few days before, "Hey, that's Step Three!" This had never happened before.

Fast forward to today, I lead a small group in the evening on every second Friday. I call this The Twelve Steps and Zen Koans or 12 & Zen for short:

http://12stepsandzenkoans.blogspot.com/

This not an AA meeting and is open to anyone. It's a non-traditional way of sitting with koans, where we allow the koan free access to the Steps.

Marvelous discussions happen.

Not limited to our small group, no matter where you live, it's a technique that's entirely portable. I invite you to give this a try – see where it takes you.

In January we sit with Step One, February Step Two, etc. We sit with the Step for five minutes. Then I give the group a koan where we sit with the Step and koan for 20 minutes. Afterwards we have discussion.

Here are a few examples from my blog:

- Step 2: Came to believe that a Power greater than ourselves could restore us to sanity.

Koan: Dogen said, "To believe in Buddhism* is to believe one is inherently within the Way." *

* Or God or AA or ...

Isn't it interesting how beliefs do not require any fact-finding or solid evidence; they're multi-layered, sometimes fleeting, from the trivial to the profound. We simply find ourselves believing something (or not believing something). In a way, not believing is a kind of believing.

Has anyone reading this never changed his or her mind on a subject? Never changed from believing this to that? Believing is fluid, it can happen in a millisecond. With Step Two, the "came to believe" doesn't have to happen before going to Step Three. Just saying there is a possibility that I might come to believe is good enough for today.

What we learn about this Higher Power thing from the Big Book, in order for it to work, the HP has to be (1) larger than ourselves and (2) outside of ourselves. We get into trouble when we play God.

- To believe in Buddha,

- To believe in God, (Big Book page 164: "Abandon yourself to God as you understand God.")

- To believe in any power greater than ourselves,

- To believe in AA…

…This is what can restore us to sanity or, if you choose, restore us to right thought (from the Eight-fold Path). Come to think of it, probably we all could use a daily dose of restoring. It's an ongoing process –

to restore us to an acceptable level, a level that is helpful to others.

- To believe one is inherently within the Way.

I had to laugh about how I first read this statement, thinking about how I was when I was out there; I was inherently in the way of most everything I did. But it reads "...within the Way," I think, basically means going with the flow, because we are the flow.

We've all been born human. Something much bigger than we was present and working during the birthing process. The only thing the mother can do is *react to* the elements of giving birth. We were within the Way then, and are still within the Way today. Every minute of the day, every second of the day, aren't we being reborn?

Whatever this "Way" is working in my life; this is what I've come to believe in; it's the way things are right now. And at the same time realizing there is no separation between me, and the Way.

- Step 5: Admitted to God, to ourselves, and to another human being the exact nature of our wrongs.

Koan: Step by step in the dark—if your foot's not wet, it found the stone.

~ Shaku Soyen

I see movement here in both the koan and Step 5.

- In the koan it's dark, we're not sure where we are going…but we are moving -- only to realize that our foot is not wet anymore!

- In going from Step 4 and now working Step 5, we are also moving. Those who never finish Step 4 remain in the dark – those who complete Step 5 move beyond the dark, toward freedom.

- Eventually completing our Steps (I know, I'm jumping way ahead), we come to realize, now we own our history instead of that history owning us.

Remember the last time, crossing a creek, when you accidentally slipped off the rock? Plunge! Instantly from dry to frigid wet! For the moment, there's no going back to dry. The universe has a wet foot.

The opposite may be happening when our sponsor says it's time to go onto Step 6. The dark and drenched feeling of Step 4 has been lifted by working Step five -- as if reaching high ground, high, dry, solid ground.

I asked D.H. to write down some thoughts from yesterday's 12 & Zen meeting: "For the week before the meeting, I found myself trying to "sit" with the step and the koan. It was a disjointed experience, as if I couldn't piece together the parts of a puzzle, despite knowing that, in truth, the parts did fit together. So I wasn't at all sure where the meditation on Friday night would take me ... if anywhere.

At the start of the meditation Bill referenced Step- 4 -- the inventory we make of the "darkness" of our drinking and using lives. As I began my meditation, the reference to step 4 seemed to become a springboard. As my meditation deepened I experienced a recognition that for years into my sobriety I was "doing" steps 4 and 5 around the darkness of my history -- dealing with the Post Traumatic Stress resulting from childhood sexual and physical abuse, with my discovery of drugs and alcohol, and with 26 years of acting out and becoming, in effect, the abuser of myself.

As I moved through the meditation, it seemed as if the koan became a moment-by-moment, breath-by-breath guide. I was able to acknowledge being with the darkness (perhaps observing it is a better explanation) without dipping my foot into it (my foot did not get wet). And so in each moment and with each breath I found the stone on which to safely plant my foot."

This same koan, coming from a different perspective brought a smile to my face.

Step by step in the dark = Do the Steps!

-- if your foot's not wet, = If you've stopped drinking and using,

it found the stone. = Life will get better.

The more I sit with this koan, the more it seems to fit any Step. Give this koan a try with all the Steps. Keep it handy. More will be revealed.

• Step 7: Humbly asked Him to remove our shortcomings.

Koan:

**how beautiful
through the torn paper screen
the Milky Way**

Issa

What is torn for you? What do you see when looking past your "torn-ness"? We come here torn up. The fabric of our "self" is torn apart... hitting our bottom. But it's through this tear, even because of this tear, where recovery and healing begins.

With Step 5 we pray, "Take away my difficulties…" Step 7 is also about doing, an action verb; we are asking our Higher Power to remove our shortcomings. This is where we find relief. By doing this, we are also building our faith in our Higher Power…our Milky Way.

When we met last Friday, here is what others said about Step 7 and this koan.

- "Looking beyond the tears in my screen; with the screen being my shortcomings and the untidiness in my life."
- "With a paper screen I only see the shadows, my character defects. The tear lets me see things in the light."

- "Low self-esteem is my character defect."

- "The paper screen is my shortcomings. Through the hole (tear) I can see a better way (the Milky Way). "Take the whole screen away!" A paper barrier is better than a rock barrier, I suppose."

- "Moving from wounded to wholeness, gratitude to appreciation, broken me to me the whole person, in awe of the universe – wholly participating in the Universe."

- "Shortcomings come from my shortsightedness. I'm moving from a place of separation to connectedness."

- "I have a filter that doesn't see the good things. I turned this koan around. The Milky Way, through the torn paper screen, how beautiful. Being sincere and going about our lives in a humble way is a good place to be when asking God for help."

- "Step 11: Sought through prayer and meditation to improve our conscious contact with God as we understood Him, praying only for knowledge of His will for us and the power to carry that out."

Koan: Only listen to the voice of pines and cedars when no wind stirs.

This koan comes from the story of Ryonen, a remarkable woman Zen teacher, living in 17th Century Japan. Commemorating when Master
Hakuo accepted her as a disciple, she wrote this poem on the back of a mirror:

In the service of my Empress I burned incense to perfume my exquisite clothes,
Now as a homeless mendicant I burn my face to enter a Zen temple.

When Ryonen was about to pass from this world, she wrote this poem:

Sixty-six times have these eyes beheld the changing scene of autumn.
I have said enough about moonlight,
Ask no more.
Only listen to the voice of pines and cedars when no wind stirs.

The other day I read a piece about Christian meditation techniques, where it said the word meditate or meditation is mentioned only twenty times in the Bible. It explained meditation as a cognitive process, "…focusing on biblical thoughts and reflecting on their meaning." This is my understanding what the writers of the Big Book meant, too – meditation was to reflect upon. Today, just as we choose our own Higher Power, we also choose our own kind of meditation, something that suits us. Meditating with Zen koans in a non-traditional way, as we do here, is one of countless varieties of meditation practiced by our twelve step members. The choice is yours, the 11th Step suggests doing it.

I often say at meetings, "I can't listen when I'm talking," and the same is true in Step Eleven. I absolutely have to say my prayers, and equally important, I must listen. This got me wondering -- what if Step 11 began with, "Sought through prayer and listening?"

What are my distractions? Mostly everything in my head ... my thoughts and the stories I tell myself. These are the winds in my life. "Only listen to the voice of pines and cedars when no wind stirs." Sought through prayer and listening...

Have you ever ridden in a hot air balloon? This koan reminds me of when I took a balloon ride. I had do idea what to expect. First, there's the deafening noise of the burning propane, blasting hot air to fill up the balloon. When all was right with the balloon pilot, and we had reached suitable altitude, he turned the propane off. Instantly it was quiet...pure quiet. It was even more amazing to experience the balloon (and us) moving above the landscape and not feeling any breeze against my face. No resistance. Then I realized it was because we were traveling exactly the same speed of the wind. How could we do otherwise? We were literally riding the wind. We were experiencing what the wind experiences. No resistance, we were in harmony with the present conditions. We were balloon.

The wind is always a part of my life whether I feel it or not. The wind of chatter in my head, the stories I tell myself, the distraction from whatever is happening at the moment. And when riding aloft it was just balloon – when no wind stirs, just the voice of pines and cedars. When no wind stirs, just my Higher Power and listen to... Whatever needs to be heard will be heard.

These koans have their way, no matter how we sit with them. A friend has been pretty stressed out from work for a while. When he heard the koan we were using, not much happened. Then it began appearing at unexpected times. Just waking up, his mind already lining up all sorts of errands and places to go in the day collapsed into "...the voice of pines and cedars when no wind stirs." He laughed, took a breath, and noticed the pine tree in his backyard.

In the book *The Hidden Lamp*, Wendy Egyoku Nakao writes about Ryonen (who burned her face with a hot iron in order to be admitted into a Zen temple) and asks us, "What would you be willing to sacrifice in order to awaken and find freedom?"

And so, as usual, we practice this in all our affairs...

Nina C. sent this about her experience, this 12 & Zen project, and what we are doing together and via the Internet, and its effect (koans and the Steps) on her life.
"thank you bill for tugging at my sleeve....koans from last year visit me often. it is nice to be with them....and sometimes too, they are like a stone in my shoe.

i have not been meditating and don't seem to care or worry about it. a seed has been planted in what seems right now a reluctant soil. "how's that workin for ya   an old sponser used to say of my   perhaps poorly chosen behaviors" she knew i was not a quitter...but more, just habituated to the comfort of my bad habits.

     so it goes. However, koans are tucked in some hidden place in me   and/or emanate from seemingly random stimulus (usually the beauty of nature or art)....and then move with me and i with them....it is really consoling how much less lonely i feel when one of them arrives....i feel kinda like i did when i had imaginary friends for whom i would make tea, save a space in my bed or pray when they were having trouble.... a little "ahhhh" happens. nice.

     my mom is still battling cancer. it has been three tumultuous years now living with a woman I don't like, yet somehow can find ways to admire......when teachers speak of the transitory and irrefutable beauty of life or the fact that a thing holds its opposites as well ..it helps me to   see the bigger picture of her and me. i live so" close to the intimate and constant hard requirements of advocating for a delusional stubborn and very angry 90-year-old woman that i forget   we are part of something else…and even in our uglier moments (which happen frequently when our wills collide or our feelings get hurt and egos race forward to protect their interests) there is   something tender sweet   laughably human about our sad little treacheries. It feels   living with her   like we are both on a rollercoaster ride. I want to puke, refuse my ticket, grip the rail, hunker down on the floor as low as i can get, evacuate my seat. I did

not design the ride but i did chose to get onto it...so...
I am learning a lot. It is rich, but feels at times more
demanding than I can meet. We forge ahead.

      so. i write as i do   to say how it is here. Koans
do a lot to help me. Unlike other many other
dialogues they allow me the fullness of time and space
to build with them a new way of seeing and being   or
ignore them or fight with them   or....there is great
relief in having the possibility of relationship with
something kind and open   not agenized and very
elastic and forgiving . i need courage and koans give
me that. so there it is.   i am not up for much more
socially than helping my mom, taking care of what our
days require and visiting with koans and other poetry i
read. (check out mary oliver if you have not
already...she is both zen   and christian. and artist
...like that one zen monk whose name i cannot
spell)...so, once again, ONE has sent what I need
zen and poetry together to help me just be ok with it
all. and sometimes to also remember the possibility of
joy.

    hope you are well. see you on the second
friday...thank you for patience warmth non-judgment
and glee...

    -wobbly zen student of what if and
howsthatworkingforya?" N.C.

Comments

Self-centeredness is at the root of our problems and our opinions and judgments have a way of keeping us in this state. The way we look at things is a huge message throughout the Big Book, finally at the end warning us about "contempt prior to investigation". In the Preface I invited your curiosity to accompany you while investigating this Buddhists in AA matter.

All of this is a lesson I had to be reminded of – curiosity opens up my world way more than my opinions do.

The birthday coins many of us carry do <u>not</u> say, "To Thine Own Opinions Be True." The coins read, "To Thine Own Self Be True," a positive statement for any spiritual practice.

The pathway to finding a Higher Power (or higher power) of your own understanding is <u>always available</u>, barred only by our opinions and judgments.

We have a nasty disease. Over the years I've seen some people stay and a lot of people disappear. Through my observations and experience, most of the people who stay in AA find their lives get better; the people who leave, their lives get worse. One reason I continue to go to meetings is to hear what happens to people who stop going to meetings. Not only do we all suffer from a common malady; we also find a common recovery in the most diversified ways. To get out of our "self" we help others. In doing this, we find that we can "forget the self," as Dogen said. When we are considerate of others, we help our "self."

To the doubters who were skeptical, I hope a new path has opened up for you; to others I hope this book has enriched your practice; and to the still unconvinced, may you find recovery at other venues. As I mentioned earlier, AA isn't the only way to find sobriety; but it is definitely one of the pathways.

To Buddhist and the like-minded alcoholic, I hope I've shown you how Buddhist practice thrives in AA. To the non-Buddhist alcoholic, this little book shows yet another example of AA's welcome availability to all.

Above all, my readers, may you find your true self in recovery.

In gratitude: Where the glass is half full even when it's empty.

The Author: Bill K. (72) lives north of San Francisco. He got sober in 1986. In 1996 he walked into a local zendo and felt right at home. Married 48 years, he and his wife have two sons and three grandsons.

Comments From Others

Thank you, Bill, for your wisdom, experience, and effort! This is a lovely addition to the tradition, and I know will be of help to many. -- Megan Rundel, Ph.D., Clinical Psychologist, Zen Sensei

In, "Three Buddhists Walked into an AA Meeting..." Bill K. shows that though the AA movement arose within a Christian context, it is not averse to Buddhist practice. He shows how early AA pamphlets were conversant with the Buddhist path. At root, this book is about occupying, owning, paying attention to your life, and getting sober. Zen and AA are both about your life, receiving and perceiving life as it rises to meet you moment by moment. But, it always comes down to the work. Can you lean into life, into the unknown and uncertain? Do the work, wake up, get sober. This book shows how Buddhist alcoholics do it. -- Rev. David Parks-Ramage, Sensei, *Open Door Interfaith Zen, Santa Rosa, CA*

A Teacher Writes

When Bill K. asked me to write something for his book, I found myself reticent. I do not think of myself as a Buddhist, though, until about 10 years ago, for the previous 30 years, I did think of myself as a Buddhist. I do practice and teach Zen, but one of the fundamental principles of Zen is no reliance on tradition or scripture, and for me, at this point, that would include no reliance on 'Buddhist' tradition or scripture.

I am also not, nor ever have been, a member of a twelve-step group. I did work as a therapist in a drug treatment program for people with opiate addiction, heroin and the like, which I did for 25 years. Through that experience I have spent a significant amount of time with people who were members of various kinds of 12- step groups and I am familiar with the 12-step philosophy.

In the end, what I found best qualified me to write something for Bill's book is that I have known Bill for over 20 years and practiced Zen together with him. Our practice together was and continues to be the occasion for many conversations about his Zen practice and his 12-step practice and how they overlap for him. It is in that context that I can say that I have found that it has not been a problem for my practice with Bill, or my practice with any other 12-step practitioner. As I used to tell my patients at the clinic, we are doing the same kind of work that I am doing with people in my private psychotherapy practice, as well as with Zen students. We are all addicted to something. We do things that are not in our best interest, knowingly. Those things can be mind habits or body habits. They can involve states of mind, or chemicals taken into the body, or activities carried out with the body, that do not serve us. We wish we did them less, or not at all. Unfortunately, for the patients at the clinic, they had an unhealthy habit that involved an illegal substance, the rest of us generally don't have that particular difficulty, but the suffering is no less. Buddhism and Zen are not for everybody, neither is a 12-step program. At this point, after practicing meditation for 40 years and teaching meditation for 20 years, I can say that the mixing of a 12-step program with a Buddhist, or Zen, meditation practice has worked for a number of people. You might be one of them, there's only one way to find out.

    David Weinstein, Roshi
    Senior Supervising Teacher
    Pacific Zen Institute
    Director of the Rockridge Meditation Community